Fire Service Leadership

The Solution to All Problems in the Fire Service.

Joshua S. Chase

Copyright © 2022 Joshua S. Chase

All rights reserved. No part of this book may be reproduced or transmitted in any form or by any means, electronic, mechanical, photocopying, recording, or otherwise, without prior written permission of the author as provided by USA copyright law.

Published By: Joshua S. Chase
ISBN: 9798831773521

DEDICATED TO

All the firefighters who strive to do their job daily and do it well.

INTRODUCTION

I feel like the we over complicate the fire service most days. Simple concepts suffice for a big portion of what we are called to do. The following pages will give you some insight into what you need to be doing to have a long and successful career in the fire service. Brothers and sisters, it's not rocket science. It's the fire service and you took an oath to do one thing...

Chapter One

DO YOUR JOB.

DO YOUR JOB.

DO YOUR JOB.

DO YOUR YOUR JOB.

DO YOUR JOB.

DO YOUR YOUR JOB.

DO YOUR JOB.

DO YOUR JOB.

DO YOUR YOUR JOB.

DO YOUR JOB.

DO YOUR JOB.

DO YOUR JOB.

DO YOUR JOB.

DO YOUR JOB.

DO YOUR YOUR JOB.

Chapter Two

DO YOUR JOB.

DO YOUR JOB.

DO YOUR JOB.

DO YOUR JOB.

DO YOUR JOB.

DO YOUR JOB.

DO YOUR JOB.

DO YOUR JOB.

DO YOUR YOUR JOB.

DO YOUR JOB.

DO YOUR JOB.

DO YOUR JOB.

DO YOUR JOB.

DO YOUR JOB.

DO YOUR YOUR JOB.

Chapter Three

DO YOUR JOB.

DO YOUR JOB.

DO YOUR JOB.

DO YOUR JOB.

DO YOUR JOB.

DO YOUR JOB.

DO YOUR JOB.

DO YOUR JOB.

DO YOUR JOB.

DO YOUR JOB.

DO YOUR JOB.

DO YOUR JOB.

DO YOUR JOB.

DO YOUR JOB.

DO YOUR JOB.

Chapter Four

DO YOUR JOB.

DO YOUR JOB.

DO YOUR JOB.

DO YOUR YOUR JOB.

DO YOUR YOUR JOB.

DO YOUR JOB.

DO YOUR JOB.

DO YOUR JOB.

DO YOUR JOB.

DO YOUR JOB.

DO YOUR JOB.

DO YOUR JOB.

DO YOUR YOUR JOB.

DO YOUR JOB.

DO YOUR JOB.

Chapter Five

DO YOUR JOB.

DO YOUR JOB.

DO YOUR JOB.

DO YOUR JOB.

DO YOUR YOUR JOB.

DO YOUR YOUR JOB.

DO YOUR JOB.

DO YOUR JOB.

DO YOUR JOB.

DO YOUR YOUR JOB.

DO YOUR JOB.

DO YOUR JOB.

DO YOUR JOB.

CONCLUSION

This book was obviously more of a novelty item. However, the concept is true. We severely over complicate the fire service most days. Take ownership of your career, stay engaged, make every effort not to quit and DO YOUR JOB.

ABOUT THE AUTHOR

I've been in the fire service for almost 17 years. Before being promoted to Lieutenant in 2020, I spent the majority of my career at the informal level of leadership. I enjoy anything that pertains to fire service leadership. My mantra at work is simple "Do your job." Do the job you took an oath to do, and it's all good. I also obviously write fire service books and speak on fire service leadership.

In 2019 I received the Fire Service Medal of Honor for making a grab during a two-alarm apartment fire. I never joined the fire service to get medals, but that was a great moment in my career and something cool for my wife and kids to be a part of. The kid visited the station later that year and made a full recovery. That was better than any medal they could have given me.

CHECK OUT MY OTHER BOOKS:

Jump Seat Leadership: The Guide to Informal Leadership in the Fire Service

Leadership at the informal level is becoming a lost art in the fire service. We lack men and women who are willing to lead regardless of their current position. Preparing yourself to lead at the informal level starts now, today. You may not carry a title, but it doesn't mean you can't influence others around you.

Jump Seat Leadership: The Lead Yourself Workbook

This workbook is the perfect companion and follow up to Jump Seat Leadership: The Guide to Informal Leadership! In this workbook we get into what it takes to lead YOURSELF in the fire service. We'll work through some tough questions so you can map out a solid plan and lead yourself well.

THIS BOOK IS PART OF THE "DO YOUR JOB" LEADERSHIP SERIES. CHECK OUT THE OTHER TITLES IN THE SERIES.

THECHASECOLLECTIVELLC.COM
Available on Amazon.com

Made in the USA
Middletown, DE
10 October 2022

12388256R00057